MOON PEARLS

REALITY OF LIFE

VISHAL B. GOLA

Made with ♥ on the Notion Press Platform
www.notionpress.com

'In this whole universe somehow and somewhere we have something for someone or something similar to someone.'

Since the age of eleven, I have experienced so much in this materialistic world and somewhere deep in my heart: my own 'Spiritual World'. I belong to a middle-class family that is not just a complicated part of our society but also plays an important role in someone's materialistic and spiritual growth. Now in my case, I have everything necessary for a good life, a not-so-big house but a 'my home, sweet home type house in which I live with my parents, a private sector hardworking employee, a simple but enthusiastic mother and housewife, mischievous younger brother, grandparents, *Chacha Chachi* and their children.

Here I'm going to dedicate this book to each member of my house. Because in my view or my perspective, the whole world lives in my home. From my grandparents to my younger cousins, they all are not just a part of our middle-class family but also represent every kind of social mentality, behavior, characteristic, and psychological and spiritual perspective. Like my grandmother, who is a devotee of lord Shiva, my mother loves Ladoo Gopal as her child, and I feel a deep connection with Goddess Durga. So technically under one roof, all different people with different mindsets are living.

When you people read my poems, you will know that the issues I have covered or mentioned in flowery terms are very familiar and part of your daily (day-to-day) life. And the reason behind my flowery language is very simple 'we are part of a society where we all try to exaggerate our pleasures and pain. We all never see the actual things or facts, and always try to hide our real emotions behind the veil of something else. 'So, as I am doing. Showing you the 'Reality of Life' in metaphorical terms.

And last but not least, I just want to add that – *'It is our beauty to present the world's most negative or unpleasant emotions with a smiley face.'* This book is dedicated to all youngsters and people of all kinds of fields. I hope you all people will try to understand the meaning and depth of each word. It is my first attempt to fill your heart with your TRUE EMOTIONS.

Contents

1. Real Me!

The real me awake, when a child is born
The real me rises, when a child rises,
The real me play, when a child is being played with,
The real me lives, when a child is shrieked,
The real me reads when a child is read,
The real me love, when a child is loved,
The real me listens, when a child is being spoken to,
The real me calms down when a child is sleeping,
The real me enjoys it when a child is enjoyed
The real me is sad, when a child grows,
The real me is anxious, when a child becomes quiet,
The real me is confused when a child lies,
The real me is stressed, when a child hides,
The real me is broken, when a child cries,
The real me is angry, when a child fights,
The real me is forgotten, when a child gets lost,
The real me is lost, when a man comes,
The real me hides when a man shouts,
The real me runs, when a man awakes,
The real me cries when a man laughs,
The real me!

*One day, I reached into my heart but there was no noise of
memories,
And now....
The real me is dying, when a child had dead!*

2. It's Me.

I can't act like others,
I can't talk like them,
I can't behave like those who hurt you always.......
I am nothing but
Just a flow of wind. I am....
so don't think about what is in my mind for you...
Because...I have nothing
Till I don't feel from my heart's depth!
Sometimes it's hard to understand me,
Sometimes it's easy to explore myself,
Sometimes I act like a child...
Sometimes I need a CHILD...
Sometimes I become miserable,
Sometimes I solve your puzzles...
Sometimes that puzzle is me...
Simply PLAY your TURN instead of...
SOLVE me; don't compare me with others...
You will receive nothing... because, at long last!
You'll have to choose another.. So...
Don't make an effort to flip your heart...
It's just me... and I'll always be just me.
No matter how many SHADES I have,

No matter how many times you've COLORED me,
You've got nothing! But try to flow with RAINBOW of my
soul…
Then you will get your SHADES in it.
I am ME I can't change….
The truth is! I have already CHANGED.
You are unrivaled; no one can compare to you…
You are unique…
You are loved…
but LOVE is not yours…
until you accept IT.

3. Re-Born from Ashes

The higher you fly…
Higher difficulties you'll face,
The deeper you go…
Deepest fear will scare you,
It's hard for everyone,
To achieve a higher self
It's hard for everything,
To attain its higher state
Tears will shed from your relations,
Eyes will burn in every situation,
Storm in my heart will throw out
Your faith,
Roots of credence will fall,
The shadow of beloved will not be there when you enter in your
sorrow,
Death will come, you will die
Your ASHES will give you a new day BRIGHT
You are not alone; you are not the only one seeing the peak of
loneliness.
The darkness in your life is just the beginning of a new ERA,
You will get back your crown
It's a transformation, it's a change, don't be scared,

It's here to give you courage,
No matter how hard it is…
No matter how many times you have cried…
Just give silence to your soul,
Just give a moment of realization,
Just give a pinch of a smile,
DEATH is not here to send you to sleep,
NIGHT is not here to give you freak,
It's a time; it's a place,
it's the moment of your life,
when you will get the biggest GOD surprise.
With tears of guilt, accept this.
With a smile of love, accept this.
No one can love you,
No one can harm you,
No one can protect you,
No one can save you,
Realize the reality….
Face the TRUTH!
When you were in a blood CAGE,
Your eyes were closed; an Ocean of sin was engulfing you,
There your loved one had kept you.
You had been living there for nine months,
So who was there to nourish you
Who was there to protect you,
That 'WHO' is also here, sitting just beside you.
Watching you, supporting you.

The only difference is
That time he was just behind you but now he is standing within
you.
You are not a weak person,
You can cross this SAD River,
Just don't try to do it yourself…
The only thing you have to do…
Just pick each leaf of your faith one by one…
Step by step,
Offer your burden on HIS feet,
REMEMBER!!
To fly in the sky, a butterfly waits so long in dead CELL,
It changes itself from life to stone ….
Wait until its time does not come and then it flies away forever.
No month, no day, no year, no time is unlucky for you,
The moment of your SORROW is the exit of burning HELL,
GUILT of sins is Cold entrance of your NEW LIFE…..
Be patient, be humble…your anger will light a DEATH NOTE
for your own…
COMPARISON will become slow poison,
SUICIDE will become self-destruction…
In this universe, so many DEVILS are there who
Will cry for a moment but some souls…
will burn from INSIDE for you.
Your DEATH NOTE will send you in a quiet wood
But
Stop the wheel of time for some good.

4. Moon Pearls

What is love?
I asked her once
She smiled
And pointed to her dress
Silk gown over Parijat's bed
Moon pearls were hanging over that
A drop of snow was like her face
I do remember her fragrance
Lavender, rose, and jasmine
Shreepankaj was reflecting on her hand
Passionflower is just like her breath
Warm blood made her an enchantress
Not from heaven
But somewhere else
She had come
To take my sense
Just like voodoo and spells
Powerful was her impact
Eternal flame and Curse of Death
Before she seemed like an insane
'Heart of Ocean' was her eyes
Dark in nature as a symbol of 'wise'

Mortal lashes but an immortal smile
which was a boon of Aphrodite
so much innocence was her cleavage
could melt any men's rage
Zeus' daughter – Hellen herself
Was nothing when she came with burning sage.
I don't know why? I resisted myself
Whenever she opened her arms and called my name
Every man wanted to taste her lips
Everywhere were wrecked heart's ships.
Passion, love, and innocence
Never push her on my lust's bed
Sometimes she acted like a child
And enjoy her whole life.
Beyond the sex and touch
We were doing fun so much
Every night she cuddled with my heart
But the end of lovecame so fast.
This was her last stage
When she was holding my hand
Together we were dancing
and kissing each other, restless
Tears were dropping from her eye
like the shed of leaves dry
Unstoppable was our love
I was holding a white dove.
Heart of Ocean became white

MOON PEARLS

Suddenly new moon came out in the night
Countless attempts I did
Breathless was my queen
Moon pearls fallen down
All flowers shed out
Sorcery of my enchantress
Dissolve in my tears
Heartless was my soul
Suddenly a dove I saw
Flying high was in the sky
Then something I realized
White dress on silk bed
Was made up of pearls itself
Which could never be fade
Remain bright on every end.
Love is something that is beyond
Every boundary and every bond
It can never be fade
It is immortal just like LOVE ITSELF!

A Note For Parents

It is just a small note (a sweet but heartful essay) from children to their parents.

Now children think being a part of a middle-class family is itself a sacrifice and Taboo for them. They feel unprotected in their own houses and fight for their pseudo-freedom. Now they feel that they are living with over-protective and possessive human beings who will never allow them to do anything and if they do, then that will be most embarrassing for them. For them, their parents are good, but with ULTRA LEVEL COOL PERSONALITY ' because when they have to be mature guardians, they become a higher-level conscious of everything from chocolate bars to condoms. And when they have to be emotional, they lose their sensitivity, and just try to control, not even control; they try to engulf their children's dreams.

Today's generation wants freedom. 'FREEDOM', this word gives another level of explanation, thoughts, and imagination to their parents.

For their parents, freedom means to just live alone, work, with no interference in their life living, etc. But we have to understand that now children don't just think about games, chocolates, marriage, children or houses, etc, they also think about their family, their future children, wife, career, investment, and other things.

Most importantly, they think about their parents. I don't think that any child ever planned how he/she should kill or throw away his/her parents. They never show their love but they care about everything. No matter how arrogant your child is, he always tries to make you happy.

As you are feeding him, he also wants to feed you, but not only with rice or grain! Also, with peanut butter or something which you can't afford right now.

Whenever they dream about luxury, cars, and other stuff they always try to put you in their imagination with big, smiley faces.

It's true, as a parent, your care for them is acceptable. 'If you give a lot of water to your plant it will die and if you don't, then it will die soon, but with water, it will suffer more.' the same about your children, your love, anger, care, questions, etc can give them a right path but also can give them a weapon to kill themselves or you.

In middle-class families, people either think about the past or the future. But children want to live in the present. And that's why you argue with them. Tell me one valid reason for your argument!! You have only one. The only universal reason is, if you don't, then they will go on the wrong path, but for God's sake, think about what you are doing with them. Neither your arguments are stopping them nor changing their mind. They are just doing work like kerosene in their imagination.

In your time you do hard work. Excellent I salute you for this, but now hard work is not enough. Smartness is the only weapon that can create a difference between hard-working ox and humans.

With time, you have to change. It's not true, you neither have to change yourself nor leave them alone. You have to walk with them together, sometimes as a friend, sometimes as a teacher, and sometimes as a parent or maybe sometimes as a foe. But you have to be all characters in their lives without changing yourself.

Because if you change, then they will be lost in this huge world. You just have to improve yourself.

They are children. They need your help, but you can't be their need.
Things are a lot to say, but words are limited.

The mind can understand everything but the heart fails to explain it. Parents have solutions to their problems if they just drop their ego, their rights over their lives, and their anger and accept the reality of life that they can't become their needs and if they do, then one day, their children will dump them in the sea of emotions because that day they will not feel necessary to fill their needs!